Ultimate
SPORTS BETTING GUIDE
Secrets to consistent winning

Mustapha S. O

Ultimate Sports Betting Guide

Secrets to consistent winning

...From the Autor of the 2016 Best Seller

**"Strategic Approaches to Starting, Growing &
Optimizing Businesses"**

Comes

"Ultimate Sports Betting Guide:

Secrets to consistent winning"

Ultimate Sports Betting Guide

Secrets to consistent winning

ISBN-13: 978-1539576969

ISBN-10: 1539576965

©Copyright 2016 by Mustapha Sani O

sasgob@yahoo.com

+2348175217867

All rights reserved under the International Copyright law.

Contents

Contents ii

Introduction 1

Sports Betting 4

One bet many options 6

Sports betting body... 8

The betting proper.. 9

Laws, House Rules, Terms and Conditions on betting 11

Types of Sports betting 16

Advantages and disadvantages........................... 17

Successful Sports Betting Tips............................. 21

Short stories of some big time celebrity bettors 50

Summary... 61

References 62

Introduction

Whether we believe it or not, one of the quickest ways of making a lot of money today is by betting. Over the last couple of years, a lot of people have made tons of cash betting both big time and small time. Betting is relatively simple to get into and anybody can do it. It works by simply predicting the outcome of events, placing bets on these outcomes and cashing out (Kochan 2008 and Gambling sites 2016).

Professionals in this field will advise you that, if you are interested in engaging in this activity, you should have it at the back of your mind that in betting, winning and losing are just two sides of the same coin. What goes against you today will work for you tomorrow and vice versa (Banker and Frederick 1986).

Betting can be small time or big time. Whichever it is, the difference is obvious. While a lot of people spend the rest of their lives wallowing in the world of small time betting; only a hand full will ever make it to the big leagues and this book provides you with some secret strategies and tips that will get you into the big leagues.

A lot of individuals, groups, and companies out there provide predictions, winning combination and more. However, professionals in the field who have been betting for years will advise you that the secret to betting is nothing more that confidence, patience, discipline and research. If you possess these qualities, then you are on your way to entering the world of big time betting and winning big (Kochan 2008).

Studies have shown that, in the world of big time sports betting, there are two things that really matter:

1. The end results

2. Where you exert the most control which is on the path you take to achieve your objectives.

You do not have to beat yourself up unduly or swerve asking yourself hard questions that are inevitable. Rather, when things go wrong, you have to develop a thick skin and learn to be a good winner or a good loser. It is important that you learn from your mistakes and keep your winnings and losses in perspective. If you cannot do that, and betting becomes a source of anxiety, then betting is not probably for you. If you can keep an even keel when all around are losing their cool, then congratulations, you are well on the way to joining the big leagues (Steve 2011).

Sports Betting

What is a sport betting?

Betting is a form of gambling that involves placing a bet on the outcome of an event. The bet can also be called a wager. Sports betting is a form of betting that involves placing a wager on the outcome of a sports event. It can also be said to be the activity of predicting sports results and placing a wager on the outcome. Simply put, the main aim of sports betting is to win more money. A bet will have two possible outcomes, it is either you win a profit based on the bookmaker, or you lose your wager (Kochan 2008 and Australia Sports Betting 2016).

Betting places the bettor into an arena of risk, uncertainty and financial decision making. The combination of these factors is a great challenge for the human mind and one which can bring about unpredictable outcomes. As such, it is important for any individual who is intending to venture into this arena to have discipline and a high level of self-control if you are going to be successful, otherwise the results may be unpleasant (Australia Sports Betting 2016 and Wikipedia 2016).

One bet many options

A lot of newcomers in the sports betting arena believe sports betting is basically based on soccer games with bettors betting on the outcomes of soccer events like Manchester United VS Chelsea, Arsenal VS Liverpool and the likes. This is not entirely correct. Sports betting has to do with a whole lot more than betting on the outcomes of soccer events. Sports' betting also includes betting on the outcome of sports events like tennis, motor sport, basketball, american football, baseball, handball, rugby, volleyball, ice hockey, golf, boxing, winter sports, cricket, darts, football, snooker, table tennis, horse racing, greyhound racing, underground dog fighting, baseball, hockey, mixed martial arts, boxing etc. Furthermore, sports betting can also extend to other non-athletic events, such as reality show contests, fluctuations in interest rates, dancing competition, political elections etc.

Sporting bets can be on games, fixtures or tournament results, or on events that take place during a fixture. For example, in a football game between Manchester United and Liverpool, possible bets include Manchester United to beat Liverpool, Manchester United to win 2-1, Manchester United to win by one goal, Manchester United to be leading at half-time, and a particular player to score a goal.

Sports betting body

There are several groups working together to make up the betting body (Gambling sites 2016).

1.　　**The betting company:** this is a company that provides sports betting services. It can be called bookmaker, bookie, sports book or betting agency.

2.　　**The betting exchange**: this can be said to be a service that provides a marketplace in which odds are set.

3.　　**The bettor (popular in the USA) or a punter (popular in the UK):** This is the person or individual who places bets.

The betting proper

When you place a bet on an outcome, you are said to be backing that outcome. For example, in a game between Manchester United VS Liverpool, if you bet on Manchester United to beat Liverpool, you are backing Manchester United. If the outcome of the game Manchester United wins, you win more money. With bookmakers you can only back an outcome, while betting exchanges enable you to bet both for and against outcomes. A bet against an outcome is called a lay bet. For example, you could lay a bet against Rory McIlroy to win a golf tournament. Your lay bet wins if anyone except Rory McIlroy wins, and loses if Rory McIlroy does win the tournament (Gambling sites 2016).

One point of difference between sports betting and casino gambling is that with sports betting, the probabilities of winning are not known, they are only estimated. Unlike a casino game, where the house edge is known with certainty. Sports betting rewards patience and research, because bookmakers are only guessing the true probability of each possible outcome. While bookmakers provide accurate odds on average, good value can be found for the experienced bettor (Steve 2011 and Kochan 2008).

Laws, House Rules, Terms and Conditions on betting

There are different laws for different countries as regards to betting. These laws on betting are controlled by the Government of that country. In most countries, it is the Government lottery Commission that is responsible for regulating these laws, as such, it will be wise to check with the country in which you reside before you get involved in betting within that location.

Similarly, different betting companies and betting exchange have different house rules, terms and conditions. It is important that the bettor gets himself acquainted with this information and understand whether or not that is what he wants before getting involved with the company (Australia Sports Betting 2016 and Gambling sites 2016).

Laws on betting

Basically, there are some laws on betting that applies in most areas where betting is permitted. These laws include (but are not limited to):

1.   The person or individual who places bets must be 18 years of age or over.

2.   The betting operator must obtain reasonable proof of identify from its customers.

House Rules, Terms and Conditions on betting

With regards to house rules, terms and conditions; below are some of the key areas Professional bettors advise bettors look into before they think about getting involved with the company. They include, but are not limited to the following:

- **Cost of registration**: Some companies charge for registration while some others allow for free registration.

- **Opening single or multiple accounts**: Some betting companies do not allow bettors to open multiple accounts. It will be wise to check with the betting company in order to get your facts right before getting involved with the betting company.

- **Minimum and maximum amounts allowable**: Different companies have different amounts allowed. You should verify such information with the company before you start betting.

- **Hidden charges and fees**: Different companies have different policies. While some companies may have some hidden charges during the transaction, others may not. You should verify his information with the company before you start betting.

- **Cancelling bets**: Different companies have different bet cancelling policies. Professional bettors advise intending bettors to check with the company so you do not lose money out of lack of knowledge.

- **Maximum number of events allowed**: Different companies have different maximum numbers of events bettors are allowed bet on. Professionals advise that bettors check with the company so that they can know the permissible limit.

- **Becoming an Agent**: If you feel you are up to it and that you would rather become an agent than being a bettor, many betting companies offer individuals and groups opportunities to become agents. You should carry out a small research on the available companies that can operate within your area and get your information correct before you make any meaningful investment.

Types of Sports betting

American Football and Soccer are considered some of the most popular sporting events when it comes to sports betting. It is a known a fact that hardly a month goes by without one or two ways in which you can bet. There are several types of bets that are available to a bettor in sports betting. Below are some of the types of betting on sporting events:

- Moneyline bets

- Run line, puck line, or goal line bets

- 2nd half bets

- In-play betting

- Draw no Bet

- Handicap

- Under/over goals

- Goals in

Advantages and disadvantages

Sports is fun and a lot of people love it. Due to its appeal, recent studies have shown that a lot of people make a living out of sports betting. However, whatever has whatever has advantages also has its disadvantages. In this section of this book, we try to take a look at some of the advantages and disadvantages of sports betting.

Advantages

- Most online sports betting systems are designed in such a way that it provides simple step by step, self-explanatory approaches to betting. This makes it easy for beginners use the system and easily make profits.

- In sports betting, you can generate a great deal of revenue without having to do any physical or tedious labour.

- In sports betting, you can use a small amount of money to amass huge sums of cash by simply making correct predictions and betting on them.

- In most countries, the profits you get from sports betting are tax free

- Sports betting is good for people looking for a second income stream. This revenue can then be channelled for savings towards things like retirement, holiday, school fee for your kids, etc.

Disadvantages

•   Being can lead to poverty and frustration: A bettor can easily spend more than he or she can afford to spend and eventually use up his entire savings. This mostly occurs when you did not do your calculations correctly or you are trying to win all the money you have lost in one single bet.

•   Betting is a very time consuming task: If you want to be a successful bettor, you must dedicate ample time researching on the team you want to bet on. You also have to spend ample time researching on the teams they will be playing against. It is important because it will help you make better predictions. Failure to do this may result in huge losses over time.

•   Sports Betting is very addictive: If it is not properly managed, can lead to lack of financial growth and extreme poverty. Professionals advise that if you are going to really succeed in betting, you must have to inculcate proper planning and allocate resources appropriately. This can be done by betting safely and allocating a specific amount of money with which you want to use in betting. Similarly, the money you win from the bets should be used wisely be spending only a small amount to reinvest in new bets and using the remaining bulk for your savings and general needs.

• Trust issues: It is a known fact that the internet is largely unregulated, as such, it is sometimes difficult to know which Sports betting providers one can trust.

Even though Sports betting is fun, it is easy to get into with so many advantages, before we get involved in online sports betting, the systems need to be tested and tried so that we can be rest assured that we are not giving out cash o fraudsters. In addition, the bettor needs to get advice from experienced sports bettors who have good knowledge about the subject matter. By doing this, it helps the bettor achieve a high degree of success, improving his chances of making successful predictions and making more money.

Successful Sports Betting Tips

Before we explore some Successful Sports Betting tips in this section of the book, we need to first ask ourselves one very important question... Why do most people bet on sports?

Previous studies reveal that people like to bet for some of these reasons listed below. They include (but are not limited to):

• Because they believe it is an easy way out to easily make a lot of money for oneself.

• Because a lot of people love sports. They enjoy competition through a safer medium of sports. They like to select their favourite teams based on their location or some attribute they feel they share with the team so they can celebrate when they win or support one another when they lose.

• Because most people love to gamble for fun and entertainment.

Research has also shown that most people would rather bet on their favourite teams to win. This is because it makes watching the game more exciting for them. There are a small percentage of people out there that actually take their sports betting very seriously; these are the people that put in the most effort and find the most success (Steve 2011).

No matter which type of bettor you are, you'll obviously be happier if you win rather than lose. There's no way to guarantee a win, but there are steps you can take to enhance your chances winning and of making some more money. To make things easier for you, this package is designed and developed via thorough research and tips from some of the most successful bettor in the world to help you achieve a high degree of success.

While most of these strategies are straightforward, both beginners and professionals alike will benefit from reading through them. You may even discover something you never knew before. Either way, this research helps you achieve a high degree of success and make more money in sports betting.

1. Get yourself prepared and organised before you start

Professionals advise that if you are going to get into betting, you should consider it as if you are going on a trip and develop a to-do list. The things you will want to do should include (but not limited to):

• Open an account with a renowned bank solely for the purpose of betting. It is not usually a very good practice to use your future savings account for betting.

• After that, put in the amount you feel you will be comfortable betting with (whether you lose or win). This is because, if you lose you will not have much to worry about, but when you win, the better off you are.

• Study and set up as many betting accounts and channels as you can. Thoroughly explore them and keep an eye on every available free bet introductory offer you get and take advantage of all the available free bet introductory offers you get. If properly done, you can add hundreds, even thousands of dollars to your betting bank, for free, and at no risk to your capital.

• Try to ensure you have all your bookmakers phone numbers stored in your phone and spread your bets around their various web platforms.

2. How do I start and which sports betting sites do I join?

With internet becoming cheaper and more available in remote areas, sports betting online today are becoming easier and most convenient ways to place bets on sporting events than ever. However, not all sports betting sites have a very good reputation. Some are scams developed to fraudulently collect money from the better without paying. Careful research has to be carried out if you are going to select a good reputable betting site. Better still, feel free to contact us with the number provided in this package.

3. Identify Your Niche

One very important secret in betting is for you to carve out your own expert niches. Creating your own niches will give you the advantage of specialization and if you specialize for a long time concentrating on your niche, it improves your chances of making successful predictions and making more money.

Professionals recommend that you do not bet just because you are bored or because of something you just see on the television or hear on the radio. This is because; you might just be dancing to the bookies' tune by betting when the odds or any edge in an event is very much against you.

Specialise on what you know or where your instincts tell you that you can have an advantage over and evaluate their claims using the same criteria and always try to bet on your terms not the bookies' terms.

4. Do not complicate things for yourself

Research has shown that complicated bets often bring forth huge payouts, as such; you will be tempted into placing complicated bets. Life they say is a risk. A ship in harbour is safe; however, that is not why the ship was built in the first place. It is not a bad thing to make complicated bets, however, research has shown that people who often start-up in sports betting by making complicated and advanced bets often record huge losses.

Placing simple bets is a key to making successful bets as you record more success more often. So when starting out in the sports betting world, professionals advise novices to start up by making simple bets. Furthermore, they advise that as you advance in the sports betting world and start gaining a lot of experience, you can then use your newly developed abilities to strategically make complicated bets.

5. Singles versus Combos

The idea of a bettor placing more than one bet (i.e., multiple bets) at the same time on one slip is often referred to as combo betting. The more the combo you make, the larger your payoff. In the world of sports betting, combo betting may also be called accumulator.

Combo betting can be fun because when you sum up the total payoff for a successful combo hit, the amount is usually huge and quite enticing. This calculation makes a lot of bettors deluded by the desire to get rich quick. It is usually this same assessment that then makes many bettors accumulate several bets in order to make their final pay off enormous.

One study from Betdistrict (2016) reveals that a lot of bettors believe that betting on four or more bets with low odds will give a bettor better chances of winning compared to when the bettor bets on single events. It further explains that combo bets are the bookmarkers dream. This is basically because, when you accumulate several combos on a single bet, professional bettors will tell you that several people who place these bets are bound to miss out on at least one single event on their bet making them loose the entire money. By the time you then check these small amounts, over the long haul, you discover that the bookmarker is saving millions off bettors little bets.

The problem with making this kind of bets is that you need all the bets to be successful. And no matter how good your analysis is, it is usually extremely difficult for something not to go wrong in all the games you are betting on. Now that is where you lose money.

If you take a look at the last sections of this book containing bettors that have made millions of dollars from betting, you just need to put two and two together to make four. By this you realise that most of them do not put combos on their bet. They mostly bet on one or two games, bet big on their most favoured predictions and wolah!!! They are in the millions.

As such, a secret strategy used by professional bettors is not to combine too many combos. Betting on single events is the professional and profitable approach to sports betting as this is advised by most professionals as the strategy that improves your chances of making successful predictions and making more money.

6. Discipline is the key

You must be disciplined if you are going to be a successful bettor. Below are some things to keep in mind when betting:

1.   Never bet with money that you cannot afford to lose as research has shown that this has the tendency to affect otherwise a sound judgment you would have made.

2.   Be calm, keep a sound mind and learn from your past mistakes.

3.   Never keep placing bigger and bigger bets with the hope that you will win all your losses with one swipe. In most cases, the results can be devastating to the bettor.

7. Knowledge as a key to success

There is a saying that "knowledge is power". And then we have another saying that "information is power". Well, we put it this way, "knowledge is money in sports betting". This is because, the more knowledge and information you have about a particular sport, the more advantage you have and the better are your chances of winning.

Professionals advise that you should avoid betting on sports you know nothing about, and instead pay more attention and focus on the sports you know inside and out. If you keep up this trend, your chances of making accurate predictions will certainly increase. This helps you achieve a high degree of success at the end of the day and the corresponding result is that you make more money in sports betting.

8. Research, research and research

Conducting research and improving your sporting knowledge is vital to successful sports betting. Carry out research in the area of study and the more and you educate yourself more on the particular area you wish to bet, the better your chances of making successful predictions and making more money.

As you carry out more research, the more you understand, the more successful options that are available to you and the more you will be able to make better predictions and the more winning you record and the more money you will be making in the process.

There are several ways you can do your research and build your knowledge. They include, but are not limited to the following:

• Becoming a fan of the particular sports or area you wish to start betting on e.g. Soccer, horse racing, Greyhound Racing, underground Dog

Fighting, tennis, American Football, Basketball, Baseball, Hockey, Mixed Martial Arts, Boxing, reality show contests, fluctuations in interest rates, dancing competition, political elections etc.

- Watching more televised games on TV relating to that area of study.

- Listening to the radio relating to that area of study.

- Reading relevant sport newspapers, news articles and studying statistics relating to that area of study.

It is worthy of note that you do not necessarily have to pour in hours upon hours into your research daily, but it is worth spending some time keeping up to date with recent form and it will increase your chances of making a big difference to how much money you make, so any effort you put into this is likely to pay off.

Do not be afraid to stand out in the crowd

We all know that betting can be thrilling, and with the advent of online betting, it is now made easier than ever before. It is a known fact that in betting, winning and losing can have unexpected effects on the brain. If you win, you experience the positive effects. If you lose, you experience the negative effects. Research has shown that majority of people who have lost huge bets over the years and have experienced these negative effects still keep coming back for more. If you are going to make betting pay you, you need to know your own mind, learn from your mistakes, develop yourself and make up your mind never to be afraid to stand out in the crowd.

There are a lot of bettors who have lost bets (big or small) and are currently experiencing these negative effects. While some crafty fraudulent individuals are aware of this, they sit back design and develop information to misdirect such bettors with the promise that they will win more money.

Professionals advise that bettors who have lost before (big or small) should not be swayed by every write-up they read. If you have taken your time to carry out your research and if you believe you have a valid case for backing something, do not be put off by such individuals. Some of them even go the extra mile of placing these misleading information on print media and online with the sole aim of misleading the crowd for reasons best known to them. Some of them even visit betting centres with an attempt to sell these misleading information to unsuspecting bettors. So, do not be afraid to stand out in the crowd.

9. Understanding and comparing the odds

The odds available on any particular bet can vary quite significantly at any given time, or even on different sports betting sites. Based on this understanding, finding value is very important. In order to get the best possible value you should always take your time to search different sites and compare their odds at any giving time. When you get the best options, try to bet on the best possible odds.

Even though finding these odds may seem difficult at first, it is not as difficult as it sounds. It just means that you compare all the available odds before placing your bets. This is another reason why the professionals suggest that a bettor should have accounts at more than one sports betting site. If you have got a few different accounts, you just need to see which site has the best odds for any wager you are about to place and go with them. Over time, this can make a noticeable difference to how much money you win.

10.   Understand and get involved in live betting

Live betting offers some great opportunities for making good money. To put it simply, live betting involves placing bets on an event that's currently taking place. This means you have the chance to watch some of the action before you decide which bets you want to place. If you are good at analysing what is happening, then this can put you at a big advantage when it comes to making winning bets (Kochan 2008).

11.   Design and develop a good record system that works for you

Designing and developing a good record system that will do wonders for you is not as difficult as it sounds. A lot of bettors do not keep record systems; because they probably feel it is a waste of time or they have gone above that or for whatever reason they feel. Professionals advise that designing and developing a good record system that works for you can make a big difference in aiding you in making better predictions and in line make more money. One hidden secret here is that you can even use this record system you develop to start tipping services that will earn you even extra cash on your bets. If you are able to keep accurate records of all the bets you place, then you can spend some time studying and analysing your results. This can help you adjust your staking accordingly, at the end of the day, improve your chances of making successful predictions and making more money.

If you are going to design and develop a good record system, all you need to do is to design and develop a system where you will be able to record and keep track of the following information for each bet:

- What you are betting on

- What odds you have

- How much you staked

- The result and any return

If you want to be able to do some serious analysis of your betting, then you should also consider breaking your bets down into different categories. The following are some of the different ways you can categorize your bets.

- By sport.

- By type of wager.

- By event or competition.

- By confidence level.

Once you have a decent sample size this can help you gain insight into what is making you money and what isn't. Knowing this will help you focus on the type of bets that are the most profitable for you. To help fine-tune any strategies you are using, you should also record your reasons for making each of your selections.

12. Understand the terms, conditions, rules and regulations

By this we are talking about the rules one must abide in order to use a service. Professional bettors advise that it is always a good idea to be fully aware of all the relevant rules and regulations at a sports betting site before you actually start placing bets. This is especially true when it comes to claiming bonuses, as there are usually a number of terms and conditions that apply, including (but not limited to) certain betting requirements that have to be met before you can make any withdrawals. You will also want to know things like the minimum stake you can place, the maximum amount that can be won on a single wager and other specific rules that may affect you.

13.   Beware paying for tips and picks

There are lots of individuals and organizations that offer paid services for giving out tips and picks. Very few of these are worth it. There are a few out there that know what they are doing and are worth using, but there are far more that are a complete waste of money. Professional bettors advise that you focus your efforts on trying to improve your own betting skills rather than wasting your time and money trying to find someone that will do the hard work for you.

14. Place bets only bet when you are clear-headed

This might not be relevant for many of you, but unfortunately it is not uncommon for bettors to mess up a lot of their hard work by going on a betting spree when they have had a few too many drinks. This is obviously something that you really want to avoid. If you do enjoy having a drink, then it is advised that do not place any bets when having one.

15. Study, Evaluation and Re-evaluation Technique (SERT)

Like we mentioned earlier, there are a small percentage of people out there that actually take their sports betting very seriously; these are the people that put in the most effort. They understand that knowledge is money in sports betting and they end up finding the most success. One very important strategy they use and will never reveal to you is the SERT secret strategy. This is one strategy that has recorded one of the highest rates of successes in sports betting for many years now (Banker and Frederick 1986).

This strategy takes into consideration several key areas that include (but not limited to):

- Organisation

- Recruitment

- Injuries

- Home field advantage only to mention a few.

Now let us have a brief look at them.

Organisation: it is a well-known fact that good teams tend to stay good and bad teams tend to stay bad. When placing bets, professional bettors know this fact only too well and advise intending bettors to keep an eye out for better team organisations, Study, Evaluate and Re-evaluate these teams before they place their bets on them.

Recruitment and player statistics: this also plays an important role in the performance of teams in most cases. The question you should ask is who are they recruiting? What transfers are being made this season? What are their player statistics? It is a well-known fact that some kinds of players can help a team right away more than others. For example, while some players can boost the defence of the team, others have the tendency to improve the midfield while others the attacking and then the goal keeping. All these areas are important and have their role in the performance of the team as such a good bettor should make out time to Study, Evaluate and Re-evaluate the recruitment plans and strategies of the teams before placing his bet on the team.

Injuries: Injuries also have an important role to play in the performance of teams. If a team you want to place your bet on has been winning all along the season and you observe that the teams successful outing is linked to a single striker because of the high number of goals he has been scoring throughout the season. If this striker gets injured, chances are the team may not continue getting that many goals in the other matches due to this strikers injury. The non-availability of the striker may even demoralise his team mates making them perform poorer than expected. When players get injured, be it a striker, defender, goalkeeper or even a centre forward, it will be a very good time for the bettor to apply the SERT strategy before placing his bet on the team.

Home field advantage: it is a well-known fact that teams playing at home get home support. This home support usually boosts the morals of the players making them perform better. When placing a bet, professional bettors advise that the intending bettors should always check for this advantage, Study, Evaluate and Re-evaluate the team before placing their bets (Banker and Frederick 1986).

Short stories of some big time celebrity bettors

While some people are busy placing bets anything between $0.99 and $10, 000, there are some individuals who have the passion of showing off their wealth and their ability to dish out millions of dollars within seconds for the world to see.

During the time of preparing this book, we took time out to do some research on some of the world's famous big time bettors. We came up with a list of some wealthy people (some celebrities) who are not afraid to spend millions betting based on their predictions. Some of them have lost in the millions and some of them have also won in the billions. Below are some of the world's famous big time bettors (All Music 2016, Biography 2016, Esquire 2016, Sports Information Traders 2016 and Topbet 2016).

Dana Frederick White, Jr

Dana Frederick White, Jr was born July 28, 1969. He started boxing at age 17 and eventually went into business. He is currently known to be a wealthy American businessman and the President of the mixed martial arts organization Ultimate Fighting Championship (UFC).

As a business man, he frequents Las Vegas to promote the premier mixed martial arts. He is a big time bettor and this can be seen with one of the big wagers he placed in one of the past NBA Finals. He has been known over the years to be one of the biggest bettors in Palms Casino Resort as evidenced by dinner tabs costing around $20,000 plus $10,000 tips and tipping dealers around $100,000.

People will also remember his deal with Snoop Dogg, as he paid the rapper $20,000 after his Celtics lost to the Lakers in the 2010 NBA Finals (Topbet 2016 and Wikipedia 2016).

Christopher Ashton Kutcher

Christopher Ashton Kutcher was born in February 7, 1978. He is an American actor and investor who is known to run a sports betting ring. In his early life, he enrolled at the University of Iowa in August 1996. While at the University of Iowa, he was approached by a model scout and was recruited to enter the "Fresh Faces of Iowa" modelling competition. He came out first and won a trip to New York City to the International Modelling and Talent Association (IMTA) Convention. After his stay in New York City, Kutcher returned to Cedar Rapids, before relocating to Los Angeles to pursue a career in acting.

Ashton Kutcher made a surprising claim in which he fronted a large sports-betting syndicate. According to his interview with Esquire, the actor describes a sophisticated operation that was clearing hundreds of thousands of dollars per week during college football season.

His story was checked out in Las Vegas. A gambling insider noted that Kutcher might be the one featured in Michael Konik's highly-acclaimed book The Smart Money: How the World's Best Sports Bettors Beat the Bookies out of Millions (Topbet 2016, Esquire 2016 and Wikipedia 2016).

Carlos Irwin Estévez

Carlos Irwin Estévez was born in New York City in September 3, 1965. He is known professionally as Charlie Sheen. His first movie appearance was at age nine in his father's 1974 film The Execution of Private Slovik.

He attended Santa Monica High School, where he was a star pitcher and shortstop for the baseball team. At Santa Monica High School, he showed an early interest in acting, making amateur Super 8 films with his brother Emilio and school friends Rob Lowe and Sean Penn under his birth name.

He rose to fame after a series of successful films such as Platoon (1986), Wall Street (1987), Young Guns (1988), Eight Men Out (1988), Major League (1989), Hot Shots! (1991), and The Three Musketeers (1993).

Over the last couple of years, he launched a betting website that mainly concentrated on sports such as basketball, baseball, and horse riding (Topbet 2016, Biography 2016 and Wikipedia 2016).

Bryan Williams (AKA: Birdman)

Bryan Williams is also professionally known as Birdman or Baby was born February 15, 1969 in New Orleans, LA. He is an American rapper, record producer, and entrepreneur. He is the co-founder and public face of Cash Money Records, which he founded with his older brother Ronald "Slim" Williams in 1991. He is also one half of the former hip hop duo Big Tymers with producer Mannie Fresh.

Birdman is believed to be one of those bettors that Bet large on sports like Super Bowl and NBA. Although, at one time, The Cash Money CEO lost $2 million wagering that the Miami Heat would win the NBA Championship over the Dallas Mavericks. But that loss didn't mean that all bets were off. After winning $1 million in his bet for Green Bay Packers on Super Bowl XLV, Birdman tweeted that he plans to put out $5 million for the Patriots at Super Bowl XLVI, which was challenged by a betting company.

He turned that down and hasn't made a bet since (Topbet 2016 and Wikipedia 2016).

Curtis James Jackson III (50 Cent)

Curtis James Jackson III is also professionally known as 50 Cent was born July 6, 1975 in the South Jamaica neighbourhood of the borough of Queens. He is an American rapper, actor, businessman, and an investor. He is believed to have started out his career by selling drugs and at one point in time was struck by 9 bullets in a 2000 shooting. He eventually left the drug dealing business to pursue a musical career. In 2002, he was discovered by Eminem, who then invited Jackson to fly to Los Angeles and introduced him to Dr. Dre and signed him a $1 million record deal with Shady Records, Aftermath Entertainment and Interscope Records.

He is a big time bettor who at one time claimed that he followed the voices in his head" and bet in the NFC Championship Game between the 49ers and Giants and ended up $500,000 richer. Another notable wager he made was when he bet $1 million on his former Bromance partner Floyd Mayweather Jr $1M in his bout against Oscar de la Hoya. 50's faith paid off when Pretty Boy Floyd won by split decision (Topbet 2016, All Music. 2016 and Wikipedia 2016)..

Floyd Joy Mayweather

Floyd Joy Mayweather Jr. was born in February 24, 1977 in Grand Rapids, Michigan. He is an American former professional boxer and current boxing promoter. Mayweather fought his first professional bout on October 11, 1996 against fellow newcomer Roberto Apodaca, who was knocked out in round two.

He is widely considered to be one of the greatest boxers of all time. Undefeated as a professional, and a five-division world champion, Mayweather won twelve world titles and the lineal championship in four different weight classes (twice at welterweight).

He calls himself "Money" and is said to live up to it every time. If there is a big sporting event, Floyd's Twitter followers expect a photo of his bet ticket. He often places seven-figure bets on any major sporting event – from the Super Bowl to the NBA Finals.

He recently bet $5.9 million and $5 million on the Miami Heat to win both Game 7 of East Finals and Game 7 of the NBA Finals, respectively.

A seven-figure amount of money is very big for an ordinary person, but not for Floyd. This is a classic example of a low-risk, high-reward bet for a guy who makes almost $90 million a year (Topbet 2016, All Music. 2016 and Wikipedia 2016).

Summary

In summary, whether we like it or not, one of the quickest ways of making a lot of money today is by betting. While many people have lost a lot over the years, many others have also won in the millions. What separates the winners from the losers is the quality of time, effort and strategy they put in.

This book has provided several winning strategies and tips used by professionals who have won millions of dollars over the years. If a bettor takes his time to study this research properly and apply all mentioned strategies, the next time the bettor places a bet, he will be amazed at the high level of intelligence he will use in making his choices. The bettor will also be astonished that this book will also help him achieve a high degree of success by improving his chanses of making successful predictions and making more money.

References

All Music. 2016. [Online]. Available from:http://www.allmusic.com/artist/50-cent-mn0000919805/biography [Accessed 7 October 2016].

Australia Sports Betting. 2016. [Online]. Available from:http://www.aussportsbetting.com/guide/intro/what-is-sports-betting/[Accessed 5 October 2016].

Banker, L and Frederick C. 1986. Lem Banker's Book Of Sports Betting. New York: Dutton.

Betdistrict. 2016. [Online]. Available from http://www.betdistrict.com/betting-guides/singles-combos[Accessed 4 November 2016].

Biography. 2016. [Online]. Available from:http://www.biography.com/people/charlie-sheen-9481297 [Accessed 7 October 2016].

Esquire. 2016. [Online]. Available from:http://www.esquire.com/news-politics/a19449/ashton-kutcher-photos-0313/[Accessed 7 October 2016].

Gambling sites. 2016. [Online]. Available from
http://www.gamblingsites.com/sports-
betting/introduction/tips/[Accessed 5 October
2016].

Greg Gordon. 2015. [Online]. Available
fromhttps://www.quora.com/What-is-the-secret-of-
soccer-betting [Accessed 6 October 2016].

Kochan, M. 2008. Secrets Of Professional Sports
Betting. Las Vegas, NV: Cardoza Pub.

Sports Betting Acumen. 2016. [Online]. Available
from
http://www.sportsbettingacumen.com/betting-
guide/how-win-sports-betting[Accessed 6 October
2016].

Sports Information Traders. 2016. [Online]. Available
fromhttps://sportsinformationtraders.com/10-most-
influential-people-on-twitter-for-sports-bettors/
[Accessed 6 October 2016].

Steve, W. 2011. Sports Betting To Win. Petersfield,
Hampshire: Harriman House.

Topbet.   2016.   [Online].   Available
fromhttp://topbet.eu/news/top-10-biggest-
celebrity-sports-gamblers.html   [Accessed 6 October
2016].

Wikipedia.   2016.   [Online].   Available
fromhttps://en.wikipedia.org/wiki/Sports_betting[
Accessed 5 October 2016].

Wikipedia.   2016.   [Online].   Available
fromhttps://en.wikipedia.org [Accessed 6 October
2016].

<u>ABOUT</u>

Whether we believe it or not,
one of the quickest ways of making a lot of money
today is by betting in sports betting. With sports betting
(compared to other forms of betting), you can actually gain
an advantage by betting smart. This can be done by
combining your sporting knowledge with proper betting
strategy, a fair amount of work, patience and discipline.
Nonetheless, a lot people complain that the money they lose
over the long term is more than the money they gain.
They also complain that consistent winning in sports betting is
very difficult and next to impossible. This book provides
you with simple and easy to apply secrets and key strategies
necessary to be a professional sports bettor.

This book will help you continually achieve a high degree
of success by improving your chances of making
successful predictions and making more money.

Printed in Great Britain
by Amazon